THE GAME OF LIFE

Talks to Young People on its Golden Rules

By

ALBERT D. BELDEN, B.D.

Author of

Boys and Girls of the Bible, The Way to Live,
Teachings of the King, &c.

LONDON

THE EPWORTH PRESS

(Edgar C. Barton)

25-35 CITY ROAD, E.C.1

FIRST EDITION, 1934

SECOND EDITION, 1935

Made and Printed in Great Britain by
Page & Thomas, Ltd., 131 Finsbury Pavement, London, E.C.2.

To

A happy family that knows how to
'play the game'—John, Kathleen,
Joyce, and Joan.

PREFACE

THIS volume of Talks to Young Adolescents on the Game of Life is put forward in the sincere hope that it may prove to be of real value to them in enabling them to adopt decisive attitudes towards moral problems in their lives.

The writer remembers how grateful he would have been for rather more concrete guidance from his elders on these matters in his own boyhood.

The Talks have appeared in serial form in the pages of the *Home Messenger* and the *Free Churchman*, and doubtless the readers of those papers will be pleased to have them at last in volume form.

Amid the rather sad confusion of modern ideas on morality it should be a useful thing to give to children early a conviction of the sweet reasonableness of God's moral demand upon His human children. Teachers, too, may find it useful to have this kind of presentation handy to them when dealing with some specific issue.

Trusting that the book may serve such useful purposes, and with warmest greetings to my readers, I am,

Yours devotedly,

ALBERT D. BELDEN.

Whitefield's Central Mission,
Tottenham Court Road, W.1.
February, 1934.

CONTENTS.

PART I

THE SACRED TEN, AND ANOTHER

PART II

OTHER RULES OF WISDOM

PART I

THE SACRED TEN, AND ANOTHER

CHAPTER I

PLAYING THE GAME

A HAPPY NEW LIFE ! to all boys and girls who read this book. We are going to study together the Rules of Life, the rules of the greatest game of all. We shall enjoy the game as never before if we master its rules more perfectly and so really ' play the game.'

The very first thing for Christian boys and girls to realize is that God, whom Jesus taught us to call Father, does not rule by fear but by love. This was not quite realized when the Ten Commandments first came to the people of Israel, but it makes all the difference between true and false obedience as to whether we keep the rules from love or from fear. When a boy really loves his mother she does not need any longer to command him to do this or that, she has only to express her wish for him to leap to fulfil it, and sometimes his love will even anticipate the expression of her wish. So Christian people come back to the Ten Commandments in the spirit of the New Testament, seeking to understand the reason why such commands were given in order to be able to obey them eagerly and freely and not simply because they are commands.

The word ' obey ' is a very interesting word. It means literally ' to listen to,' ' to give ear to.' The boys and girls who are doing Latin will understand when I say that it comes from two Latin words ' ob ' and ' audire '—to hear. The whole meaning of the word lies in the fact that in this world there are people

13

who know and people who do not know, and it is wise for people who do not know to listen to those who do, and try to carry out what they are told.

Think, for example, of sport. When most of us come to our first games, Cricket, Rugger, or whatever they may be, we find that they are governed by certain rules. These have been fixed up by folk who understood how to make the game, doubtless many years ago, and if we refuse to obey the rules, all we do is simply to ruin the game. In a very real sense the rules are the game. It is no fun to play tennis with a racquet twice the width of your opponent's ; it is not football to shoot into your own goal and claim that you have defeated the enemy ; it is not cricket to refuse to surrender one's bat when the verdict of l.b.w. has been given.

Now the moment we understand in a matter like this we become eager to obey the rules, we see there is no fun in cheating and our obedience is not because of compulsion, but because of reason. It is free and not forced. Similarly, when we really understand these great rules of life which are called ' Commandments ' we begin to see their beauty and we want to obey them. Nothing will so keep us from temptation to break the rules of life than to study them so carefully that we really fall in love with them and begin to find them really precious to us, something without which life would become a very unhappy thing. That is what the ' rules of life ' are for, to make the game worth playing.

There was once a boy who belonged to a large Bible Class, and this class rather prided itself on the original nature of its arrangements. This boy, Dennis, took a leading part in fixing up a system of Judge and Jury, before which any fellow in the class, who was slack or did what was not quite right, might be summoned

and tried. This was quite good fun for a time and
very useful in keeping discipline in the class, only,
unhappily, one day Dennis received such a summons!
He had been so taken up with certain private affairs
that he had rather forgotten the class, and so the blue
slip summoning him to appear before the Court turned
up on his doorstep one morning. My word! he was
furious! He quite forgot that he had taken the leading
part in framing it all up! He decided he would never
go near the class again, and although he received two
or three more blue slips, for several weeks he remained
away from the class.

Then one Sunday afternoon he took a walk out into
the country, and passing a certain farm he saw a man
rifling a marrow bed, and he remembered there had
been a good deal of complaint lately from farmers about
their produce being stolen. He made his way cautiously
across the field intending to surprise the man and to
capture him, but the man was a little too clever for him,
and by the time Dennis had arrived on the spot the
man had disappeared. Unhappily, just then the farmer
turned up, and noticing the despoiled marrow bed he
at once took hold of Dennis as one of the thieves, if not
the thief, and nothing that the poor boy could say would
alter the farmer's opinion. He was taken down to
the farmhouse whilst the farmer started to ring up
the police. This threat was too much for Dennis,
and wondering what he could possibly do he at last
blurted out : ' Look here, sir, I belong to —— Sunday
School. Mr. —— is my Bible Class teacher. Will
you ring him up first before you ring up the police ? '

When the farmer heard that he agreed, because he
knew the Bible Class. You can imagine Dennis's
feelings as he wondered whether over the telephone
his teacher would disown him as a member of the class
after an absence of several weeks. When, however,

the farmer turned away from the telephone he was apparently satisfied and allowed Dennis to return home. Dennis had failed his School by refusing to play the game, but the School had not failed him. It was a very shamefaced Dennis who turned up at the Bible Class on the following Sunday, quite prepared to answer the little blue summons at last and take his gruel like a man.

There may be times when we think we can do without the rules of life, but we cannot do without life itself, and therefore we cannot really do without the rules. Here is the great secret of a really happy new Life. Now we are going to examine each one of these rules of God for right living so that we may learn to obey them with happiness and not from fear.

THE FIRST RULE—ONE GOD

' Thou shalt have no other gods before Me.'

THE TEN COMMANDMENTS were probably first given in very short sentences, and the first Commandment certainly fulfils that character : ' Thou shalt have no other gods but Me.' It must have always been very difficult to worship several gods, specially when they were gods, and sometimes goddesses, of such very different character like those of Rome and Greece, and Ancient Egypt and Babylon. No wonder the behaviour of men in such worship was very confused because, you see, we tend to become like that which we worship. The word ' worship ' really means ' worthship,' and that which we hold of most worth we insensibly copy and imitate. If we worship a god who is cruel, we become cruel ; if we worship a God of Love, as Jesus taught us to do, we become loving ; if we worship a number of gods, some cruel, some cunning and even brutal, then we become a mixture of these things, and that is very unsatisfactory. It is a sad thing to have our characters pulled in several different directions at the same time. You would feel very surprised if you went out one morning to find that one of your legs wanted to walk south and the other one wanted to walk north ! The chances are that in the struggle between the two you would come to a standstill. So it is with those who worship many gods. In fact so difficult is it to do this that you usually find among such people a tendency springing up very quickly to exalt one god above all the others.

And so humanity nearly everywhere in the world in this way moves on to the idea of there being only one true God. That of course must be so if there is to be a real God at all, because by this wonderful little word ' God ' we do mean the Supreme Ruler of the Universe, and there cannot be two or three, or half a dozen, Supreme Rulers !

Most London boys and girls will know the great district of London, almost in the centre of it, which goes by the name of St. Pancras, but perhaps they will not all know that it is named after a little lad of fourteen years of age who lived in Rome during the reign of the Emperor Diocletian, about 300 years after Jesus lived. Now Pancras had been brought up in a family which worshipped the Roman God Jupiter, and in his earlier years he heard some very strange stories about this god, stories, alas ! of cruelty and bloodshed. But at last, his parents having died, Pancras went to live with an uncle in Rome who was a Christian. His uncle took him into the catacombs, underground passages in Rome, where Christian martyrs were buried, and there he learned to love and respect the brave men and women who had given their lives for the sake of Jesus Christ.

Pancras had inherited a very great fortune, and this directed the attention of the Emperor to him, and one day this boy of fourteen found himself standing in front of Cæsar's throne where he was severely scolded for having anything to do with Christians. And Pancras there and then had to make his great choice between the false gods of Rome with their cruelty and baseness, and the one true God whom Jesus Christ called Father. The noble lad made his choice bravely, and at last suffered death for his loyalty to the one true God.

He was only one out of many, but deep in his heart there was a great joy that he could give his life in order to bring nearer the victory of God over mankind.

You and I in these days are not forced to choose between gods like Jupiter and Apollo, and Christ, but perhaps for that reason we are in danger of worshipping gods of another kind. There are those who make a god of Money, and others who make a god of Fashion, and others again who make a god of Pleasure. The false gods are always *made*, either by the human mind or the human hands. The true God has never been made, He is, instead, the Maker. Whom do you really worship?

It is possible, alas! to say that one worships the true God and yet by one's deeds and life to make it plain that we have got other gods before Him, yet we can never build the perfect character except as we worship the Perfect God.

Chapter III

THE SECOND RULE—NO IDOLS

' Thou shalt not make unto thee any graven image. . .'

THESE COMMANDS OF GOD were given all afresh to the
people of Israel by Moses in order to help them to be
the healthiest and happiest people possible, and looking
round on the other nations they were able to see what
terrible mischief idol worship did amongst them. The
people in those nations came to think that God actually
dwelt in images of wood and stone, many of them
revoltingly ugly and cruel in their expression, although
some others were beautiful and even noble in aspect.
But this sad and curious error made people think of
God as shut up to one place and one form. It obscured
for them the fact of the soul, and made the life of the
body almost everything, so that the worship of these
idols became full of cruelty and evil deeds. In some
places there were human sacrifices offered to these
mere lifeless shapes.

One of the Hebrew prophets, a great unknown,
who shared the exile in Babylon, makes good fun of
the idols of the city. He describes how they are carried
along on beasts of burden in religious processions.
They may look as though they are alive as they bow
to the multitude, only, you see, they bow because they
cannot help doing it, because of the movement of the
beasts on which they are bound. He says : ' they stoop,
they bow down, but they cannot lift,' and he goes on to
speak about the true God who is not carried but who is
able to carry.

In another place the same prophet describes how an idolater, wanting to be religious, will carefully choose a tree *that will not rot*, out of which he shapes an image *that will not totter*! So the prophet lights up the utter powerlessness of this kind of god; their powerlessness at least for help, though, alas! they were powerful enough for cruelty. So it came about that God, through Moses, forbade His people to make these things. God wanted their thoughts drawn away from outside things to the Unseen Spirit in themselves, and in later times Jesus in His full and final revelation of God told us definitely ' God is Spirit, and they that worship Him must worship Him in Spirit.'

Most of you, I expect, will have heard of the Hawaiian Islands which lie at the cross-roads of the Pacific. They are of great importance commercially and politically, but until quite a few years ago they were almost entirely given up to idolatry. Through the brave work of British and American missionaries they are to-day quite free of a custom which in its time was full of cruelty.

For the overthrow of idolatry in the Islands of Hawaii, God chose a lonely little heathen child who somehow found his way from these Islands to America. Little Henry Obookiah was sent away from the Islands to a Foreign Missionary School in Connecticut. One day, some years later, a little dark-skinned lad was found sitting on the steps of the famous Yale College crying because he had no one to teach him. The man who found him, Edwin W. Dwight, took pity on him and helped him, and this lad became at last a famous missionary to his own country, and began the American Missionary Movement to the Hawaiian Islands.

Curiously enough, before Obookiah and his party could get to work on the Island, they received news that certain famous idols had been overthrown. For some time the natives had observed that white visitors did many things that the idols were supposed to forbid, such as certain ways of eating, and yet were not punished ; and at last, two young queens, named Kashumanu and Keapuolani, began to test the power of the idols by deliberately disobeying their laws, and finding that they too suffered no harm, they at last gave orders that the idols should be destroyed. A number of the priests, who perhaps had long known that the idols had no real power, joined the queens in these reforms, and Hewa-Hewa, the powerful high priest of the War idol, openly allowed this movement, calling for the complete overthrow of idolatry and declaring there was only one Great God in the Heavens. So the temples were burnt and the idols destroyed just as Obookiah's vessel came to the Islands. This made his great work of gradually cleansing the other parts of the Islands of the same sad superstition very much easier.

We can well feel sorry for people whose lives are clouded with terror by reason of savage and degraded idolatry, but we must not forget that we, too, have our idols though they may never be shaped into images. Anything we prefer to the will and spirit of God can become so easily the thing we really worship in place of Him. As the great Apostle of Love wrote in the letter that we find in the New Testament, 'Little children, guard yourselves from idols.'

CHAPTER IV

THE THIRD RULE—REVERENCE

*' Thou shalt not take the Name of the Lord thy God
in vain.'*

THERE IS A SAYING that ' little pigs have big ears,' and
alas ! this saying is sometimes applied to boys and girls.
I know it is not a kind remark, but it is one that reminds
us that boys and girls hear a good many things, and
often things that are not good for them to hear. I expect
they have often heard people cry ' By Jove ! ' or ' By
George ! ' and, alas ! sometimes one hears them say
' By God ! ' One does not like even to print such a
sentence because of its horrible irreverence, but it is
very sad when boys and girls overhear remarks like this,
and grow up to think it does not matter how one uses
the Holy Name. Even such phrases as ' By George ! '
and ' By Jove ! ' are simply mild substitutes for the other,
and though they are not so bad, they do point back
to what is really a very bad thing. You would not like
to hear your mother's name used like that, would you ?

In the early history of religion, many years ago,
people used to think that there was a peculiar magical
power in the name of their god. They thought that
to mention the name brought the god on the scene ;
therefore they would never dare to mention the name in
a light or a joking way, or simply to express their selfish
anger. It is a sad thing, is it not, when savage, uncivilized
and ignorant people can teach a nobler reverence than
people who have all the advantage of living in the light
of Christ ?

It is this sin against reverence which this great rule of life forbids. It is a serious thing to injure one's sense of reverence by dropping into careless ways of thought and speech about sacred things, and if we thought earnestly about the deep insult to God we should be too ashamed to do it. And we must not think that it is less terrible so to insult God because we have learned that His way with us is love instead of punishment, for to insult so loving a God is a much more terrible and evil thing, and brings its own punishment in the coarsening of our nature, for such irreverence leads on to other irreverences, so folk who become careless of their speech about God open the door of their lives to still more sinful deeds.

There was once a boy named Harry who belonged to a Cricket Club. He was a boy who had always been brought up to think reverently of religion. He had a good mother and father, and the Club to which he belonged had been organized by him and another boy for the older lads of the Church that they attended. Some of the others, however, were not so careful in their behaviour, and so there was at times a good deal of swearing in the team. I am glad to say that Harry proved his quality not only by his reverence for good things, but also by his magnificent batting. He was easily the strongest batsman in the team, and more than once it was his superb scoring that turned defeat into victory for them. More than once, in Committee, he brought up the question of swearing, trying in a manly fashion to make the other fellows see what a disgusting business it was, and amongst other things he made a very sound and strong claim that a fellow who swore revealed a lack of self-control which was bound to affect his cricket.

One day, just before a very important match, something worse happened, and one of the fellows who was most prone to this nasty habit of swearing, used the name of Christ in an oath.   This was more than Harry felt able to stand, and he went to the Captain and said : ' I am sorry I shall have to do something that looks like letting the team down, but I am not going to remain a member of this Club if the name of Christ is going to be used irreverently.   You can accept my resignation straight away !   There is one thing more sacred to me than my cricket, and that is my religion.   I know what it has done for me, and I should feel a skunk if I let the name of my best Friend be used in an insulting manner.'

The Captain was in consternation, and he at once called the team together and asked them what they should do about it.   He repeated to them what Harry had said, and after a dismayed silence, the fellow responsible said in a rather shamefaced sort of way : ' We can't let Harry go, and I should feel that all the fault was mine.   I am sorry, I apologize !   If it will help the situation I will go myself, unless you are willing to accept my promise that I will not do this kind of thing again.'   Harry, of course, at once said he was willing to accept the promise, and I am glad to say that his firm stand succeeded in clearing the Club of this kind of trouble.

I do not say that one should always plunge into protest of just that kind.   It is well to choose one's opportunity, and if possible deal with the person privately and straightforwardly, but I think in this case Harry was justified in using the pull that he had, rather than be unfaithful to his best Friend.   What do you think ? Can you afford to injure your reverence ?

Chapter V

THE FOURTH RULE—THE HOLY DAY

' Remember the sabbath day, to keep it holy.'

THE PRACTICE OF KEEPING one day in the week specially
for God is a very, very ancient one. The seventh day
was so kept as far back as the days of King Hammurabi
in Babylon, 500 years before Moses, and it finds its
place in these Ten Commandments because it is such
an excellent rule of life. Doubtless people in those days
found that there were so many things in life claiming
their attention every day that it was difficult to get
enough time to think about the soul, and the true conduct
of life, or to enjoy quiet communion with God, and to
offer Him that worship which re-creates man's spiritual
power. Yet our life to-day is still more full, still more
busy, and our world is a much more wonderful world of
motor-cars, and steamships, and railway trains, and
aeroplanes, and world-wide business. So if they
needed it, we need it still more, and yet, alas ! we are
much more careless about it to-day than they were.

Christian boys and girls perhaps may be puzzled
that the day they are asked to keep holy is not the
seventh day of the week but the first. But after all,
it is not the actual day that matters so much as the
keeping of at least one day, and Christian people keep
the first day instead of the Jewish seventh day because
that day, Sunday, celebrates the most wonderful Divine
act in all history, the resurrection of Our Lord from
the dead.

A group of girls not long ago were busy in a fierce argument. A new Tennis Club had been opened in their neighbourhood which they had all joined, and the question had come up as to whether the Club should open on Sundays or not. So many of the clubs were opening and playing on Sunday, and some of the girls were arguing that with the extra practice these clubs would be bound to win in the matches. But two of the girls, Joan and Kitty, said point-blank that they would not play on Sunday. 'It is not,' said Joan, 'that we think it a wrong thing to do, so much as we feel that we have got something better to attend to, something which is really more important and urgent. You would not expect us to come and play when we ought to be at our lessons, and you have no right to expect us to play when we have on hand the still more important business of supporting our Church and attending our Bible Class.'

While they were arguing, Kitty's father came along. He was a doctor, and partly for fun the girls drew him into the argument, and he took a very interesting line. He said : 'I know how keen you girls are on sport and I think it is fine for you. It is not much good having healthy minds without healthy bodies, and I expect you are rather troubled about this idea that the girls and fellows who play on Sundays will get ahead of you in their tennis. But,' he continued, 'I think you are overlooking one important fact which I, as a medical man, can vouch for. You know that even machinery has to be stood off every now and again to give time for the metal to rest, otherwise it degenerates ; and in all things that combine and consume energy (and that is, pretty literally, *all* things) there is a principle of alternation as it is called, of effort and rest, that has to be observed, otherwise the effort becomes weaker and poorer. Now, I think that a Sunday's rest from tennis ought to make you better, not poorer players, if you put your best into it at other times. It will give time for your capacity and skill to sink into your subconscious mind, so that it becomes more automatic, and in this way give you a quicker and surer progress in the game.'

' Well, that is certainly an idea ! ' said one of the girls, ' and I vote we try it.' And the girls decided there and then that they would vote against the Sunday tennis and put this idea to the test.

But what is still more interesting is that one or two of the other girls began to ask Joan and Kitty how they spent their Sundays, and decided to spend their own in the same way.

These rules of life, boys and girls, are full of the deep wisdom of God, wisdom tested through long ages of human experience. We must not let the cheap conceit of the more ignorant of this modern age cheat us out of the best use of the best day of all.

CHAPTER VI

THE FIFTH RULE—GRATITUDE

'Honour thy father and thy mother . . .'

FOR THE HEBREWS, as for most of the strong, early races of mankind, it was part of the supreme wisdom of life to hold in good respect one's elders. You will have heard Abraham, Isaac, and Jacob referred to as ' the patriarchs,' and in the early life of most nations, the patriarchs or fathers, the wise old men of counsel and long experience, have a great influence. It should not be difficult even for small boys and girls to see the wisdom of this. ' We live and learn,' says the proverb, and it ought to be true that the longer we live the more we learn and the more we know. Undoubtedly this is the meaning to be read into the second part of this Commandment, the promise that ' thy days may be long in the land which the Lord thy God giveth thee.' Long life and wisdom go hand in hand. Wisdom means safety, carefulness, knowing the right way rather than the wrong of doing things.

Perhaps my readers will see this more clearly if they think of their own home life, and of the many times when disobedience to mother or father has brought them into trouble and sometimes into danger. A little boy who will not honour his mother well enough to obey her when she tells him not to run into the road but to keep on the path, need not be greatly surprised if he is frightened by a narrow escape from a motor-car or is knocked down by a bicycle.

Some of you will read one day Hilaire Belloc's *Cautionary Tales,* and will discover the grain of truth wrapped up in their funny extravagance. There is the story of the boy named Jim who was taken to the Zoo. He had been told to keep with his nurse, but he had a bad habit of disobeying and slipping away by himself. On this particular occasion Mr. Belloc tells us :—

> He hadn't gone a yard when—BANG !
> With open jaws, a Lion sprang
> And hungrily began to eat
> The Boy—beginning at his feet.

The Keeper rushes to help him, but—

> The Lion, having reached his Head,
> The Miserable Boy was dead !

And when his parents are told, his Mother calmly says :

> Well—it gives me no surprise ;
> He would not do as he was told !

There is, happily, the other side—we need not disobey and fail to honour our parents. If we hold them in a true love and tender regard we shall strive to follow their counsel and be guarded from many a snare and pitfall.

It is always inspiring to hear of a son following in the footsteps of a really great father. The *Manchester Guardian* is one of the finest English newspapers, with a very wonderful reputation for truthfulness and fearless courage in championing the right. Some time ago its Editor, C. P. Scott, passed away to the other life, but his son, E. T. Scott, was ready to step into his shoes, a young man whose character had been shaped very largely by the high honour in which he held his father. A deep impression was made upon the world by this splendid instance of a noble father producing a son every whit as noble.

The world recently learned about Lord Haldane, one of the finest of our recent British statesmen, that he wrote a letter to his mother *every day for forty-seven years* ! He tells how sometimes when he reached his rooms in the early hours of the morning he was so tired that he could scarcely keep his eyes open, and yet not once during that period did he fail to send to his widowed mother in Scotland a letter from her boy.   What splendid faithfulness !

It is well for every boy and girl to think sometimes a little deeply of what they owe to father and mother, to remember the patient toil of their parents on their behalf, the provision of the lovely shelter that is called home, the constant good food and clothing, and all the rich affection showered upon them. There is no sin quite so base and cruel as ingratitude, no virtue more fitting and more exalting to one's character than a rich, deep gratitude that strives eagerly to fulfil its debt of love.

No wonder we find gratitude built into these great Rules of Life.

Chapter VII

THE SIXTH RULE—SELF-CONTROL

' Thou shalt not kill.'

I CAN IMAGINE some of my little readers saying ' This Commandment is not for us. We are not likely to murder anybody ! ' and I would not frighten any one for the world by suggesting that they may. But we do need to remember that every murderer was once a child, and perhaps an innocent and good child at that. We need a great pity in our hearts for people who do this dreadful deed. So many are driven to it by swift and ungovernable passion, the fruit of uncontrolled temper and selfish anger in earlier years. Others are led into it by slowly developing greed, a selfishness which in the course of the years grows hard and cruel to a dreadful degree. Perhaps the meaning of the Commandment to you and me is that we should watch more carefully the beginnings of these things, that we should guard against any state of mind in which we wish somebody out of the way or even dead. Do you remember that Jesus Himself said once : ' Ye have heard that it was said to them of old time, Thou shalt not kill, but I say unto you that every one who is angered with his brother shall be in danger of judgement. If therefore thou art offering thy gift at the altar and rememberest that thy brother has aught against thee, leave there thy gift, go thy way and be reconciled to thy brother, and then come and offer thy gift.'

What kind of a temper have you ? Is it hot and fierce, and do you let it run away with you, so that you say things and do things for which afterwards you are deeply sorry? It is well to remember that passion often makes us do things that we cannot put right afterwards, however hard we try.

It is a sad thing to see friends drift away from people who habitually lose their tempers, and there are few things that help people so much as to meet those whose tempers are under firm control. Teachers with bad tempers have murdered the minds of their scholars; employers with bad tempers have sometimes murdered the characters of their employees. Anger is the real sin. A wise man said once: 'There have been many occasions when I have felt it right to be justly angry, only I find that I have mostly mistaken the times!'

There was once a boy, who, I am sorry to say, earned the name of 'Quarrelsome Tommy.' He had a little friend, named Susie, who determined to cure him. So she set herself the very great task of never quarrelling with Tommy. She was playing a game of cricket with him one day and bowled him out before he could make a run.

'Now you bowl me out!' she cried, running to take the bat; but Tommy threw the bat down and walked away. 'You don't play fair,' he said, 'girls never do!'

'Oh, Tommy,' said Susie, 'you know quite well that is not true, I did play fair!'

'There!' cried Tommy, hopefully, 'now who's quarrelling?'

'I'm not!' said Susie, 'what I am saying is the truth, and the truth can't hurt anybody!' And Tommy, looking at her friendly face and laughing eyes, walked sulkily away.

Susie called some other girls and boys to play with her, still keeping perfectly cheerful. Tommy met his mother coming out of the garden gate. 'Susie won't quarrel with me!' he cried fiercely, 'and she won't let any one else either. Well, they can play by themselves ! '

' I don't suppose they will mind,' said his mother, quite calmly and even happily ; so Tommy had to stand and moon about while the other children were enjoying the game.

Susie called out to him presently, ' Do come and play,' but still he would not ; and then, suddenly, while Susie was batting she hit up a very high ball which came straight to where Tommy was sulking. It was too much for him to refuse—springing into the air his hands closed upon the ball and his voice rang out triumphantly, ' Caught ! '

There was a moment's silence among the other children, and then one said, ' But he isn't playing ! ' Another said : ' It's *so* lovely to play without quarrelling,' and the third said, ' Susie, don't ask quarrelsome Tommy to play again ! '

The boy turned away, hot tears filling his eyes, but Susie was after him in a second : ' I say, that was a jolly fine catch,' she said, ' you ought to play ! '

' They don't want me,' said Tommy, hanging his head.

' Oh yes, they do ! ' said Susie, ' you do, don't you children ? '

And one by one the children said they did, and the youngest piped out, ' He 'ont qorrel any more ! ' And in this way Tommy was at last cured.

Is not that a good way of keeping this great rule of life ?

CHAPTER VIII

THE SEVENTH RULE—LOYALTY

' Thou shalt not commit adultery.'

THE WORD ' ADULTERY ' is made up very simply from the word adulterate which means to ' spoil ' or ' ruin.' It has come to mean the sin of disloyalty in a special relationship—that of husband and wife. As boys and girls are not yet husbands and wives, it is better to use the word ' disloyalty ' for this sin, and to think of the noblest of all virtues, loyalty, as the one thing above all to be cherished and guarded by us. One form of disloyalty leads so easily to other forms of it, and it is the selfish soul that is in most danger of this kind of sin. If we set up a habit of always doing what we like, what we want to do, following our own desires without reference to what they mean to other people, then we may pass on from one bad form of this sin to still worse and even terrible forms of it. It is happier for us to think of the glory of loyalty, of the friend who stands by his friend through thick and thin, who shares his sweets, his toys, in real friendliness, and who always ' plays the game,' scorns to cheat, and can lose with a smile.

Perhaps some of you have seen a very fine picture of a very well-dressed little boy who is standing in front of a table round which there are sitting some of the fierce, close-cropped ' Roundheads ' of the army of Cromwell. The boy's father was a Cavalier, a soldier of King Charles I. He had taken refuge in a secret cupboard of the grand oak parlour of his home, and it is in this very room the little son is being questioned, in the hope that he may betray his father. He is not more than five years old, and looks very small standing on a stool, his head only just showing above the table. 'When did you last see your father?' is the question that is being asked, and it is the title of the picture. But as he thought of his father the little lad's heart grew so full of love and courage that, although he knew exactly where his father was hiding, not all the threats of the fierce soldiers, nor their scowls, could frighten him into telling. To the honour of Cromwell's soldiers, we are glad to record they were so impressed by his courage and loyalty that they went away without doing him any harm, conquered by the faithfulness of a little child.

In a book entitled *Drayton Hall* there is a wonderful story of loyalty of a boy to his school chum. Frank Austin, a lad of about eighteen, a scholar of Drayton Hall, gave his life to Christ and tried to serve Him by starting a Mission in the poor district of his town. His father was an atheist, and did not believe in God at all, and he was so angry with Frank for trying to follow Jesus that he threatened to take him away from Drayton Hall and send him to a Military School. Frank was dismayed at his father's attitude, but he would not give up his Mission work.

He confided his trouble to his friend, Will Seaton— a merry, mischievous boy, leader of every wild escapade in the school. But Will could be serious on occasion, and he listened with a troubled face while Frank told his story, and then asked in a hesitating way if his chum could not do as his father wished. Frank looked at him and asked: 'Would *you* lower your colours, Will?' and instantly came the answer: 'No, I wouldn't, stick to it, old boy!' And Frank went home, fully prepared to 'stick it' even if it meant leaving the school he loved.

There was no alteration in his father's plans, he must go immediately, and the leave-taking with his mother was terribly sad—she was very far from well, and as Frank said good-bye to his father, Mr. Austin asked : ' Will you leave her like that ? ' Frank hoped for one moment that his father had relented, but found he could only stay with his mother if he would renounce Christ. So he went sorrowfully out of the house to the railway station to take the train to the Military School. He got into a carriage, and leaned back wearily, wondering how it would all end, when suddenly the door was flung open and a boy threw himself on to the seat beside him with a merry laugh ! It was Will Seaton, and when Frank had recovered from his surprise sufficiently to ask for an explanation, Will told, very airily, of his sudden decision to leave Drayton Hall and go with his chum. Frank was overwhelmed by such a proof of loyalty—that the careless, irresponsible Will Seaton should give up the School to enter upon exile with him seemed too wonderful to be true.

The Military School was reached at last, and they found it even more gloomy and prison-like than they had anticipated, and Frank realized more than ever the sacrifice his friend had made for him. Then, before a day had passed, came a telegram for Frank summoning him home immediately, his mother was dangerously ill.

In his home Mr. Austin paced the floor, watching the clock and awaiting Frank's return—and he was afraid ! He feared his wife would die before her son could reach her, and he was afraid of Frank's anger, he did not think it possible his boy could forgive. At last came the sound of carriage wheels, and Frank sprang from the cab. Before he passed to his mother's room he shook hands with his father. He was in time, and his return brought peace to his mother who recovered very quickly. Mr. Austin learned a bitter lesson, and some time afterwards he gave his own life into Christ's keeping. So Frank, through his loyalty, won through all his difficulties, and Will Seaton was always a dearly-loved and honoured friend in that home.

The finest form of loyalty is forgiveness. When others have been unfaithful, disloyal, cruel, and perhaps dishonest, the call may come to us as to whether we are going to remain loyal to their better selves, buried beneath their sin. If we can find it a joy to forgive, then in such forgiveness we shall call forth that hidden and crushed better-self back again to life and strength. This is the wonderful kind of loyalty that God has shown to us all in Jesus our Saviour. Christ loves us with a love that will not let us go, He is always loyal to our better selves. His friendship and loyalty is never ' adulterated.'

THE EIGHTH RULE—HONESTY

' Thou shalt not steal.'

ONE OF THE EARLIEST JOYS that we know in life is to have things that belong to us and not to other people. The number of boys and girls who take a delight in saying ' That's mine ! ' meaning quite emphatically ' It isn't yours ! ' Sometimes they say it angrily, because somebody else has picked up their toy or book. They are so full of this wonderful joy of possession that they can scarcely bear their brothers and sisters to handle anything of theirs for two minutes ! This, of course, can become very selfish, and if we do it too much, can make us very mean ; nevertheless it has its fine aspect. It means that we do understand how important it is that there should be a certain number of things in our life that we have to control and manage and that we can use, and through which we can show what we are made of and develop our ideals and powers.

It is not difficult for us therefore to see what an unhappy thing it would be for any one to come along at any time and just ' take what isn't his'n ! ' This does not mean, of course, that any one should have too much, and certainly does not mean that some people should have so much that other people cannot have anything at all. Where that kind of unfairness exists, and alas ! there is so much of it in the world, it is a real threat to the right condition of things, and it becomes a terrible encouragement to people who need the very necessities of life to break this important rule, and we have no right to put such a strain upon them.

So if we want this Commandment respected we must avoid the two extremes ; we must avoid the condition in which *anybody* can take *anything*, and we must avoid the condition in which *somebody* can take *everything*. Such stories as those of Robin Hood, in which most of us revel as boys, are really a protest against this second kind of mischief, but we must be careful not to take them as an encouragement to ' lift ' our neighbour's belongings ! So important is this rule, and it has been preserved by humanity for so many ages, that it has become built into our conscience and few of us could now steal without giving something like a shock to our being.

I remember so well a story of a boy named Harry, who, when he was at school, robbed a cherry orchard. I believe he gave himself rather a pain with the fruit ! But that was not the only pain he suffered, because a very mischievous school-chum saw him do the deed, and collected the cherry stones afterwards ! Then, while all the school were asking who the thief was, because the Head Master was very interested, this rather cruel boy kept planting the cherry stones on poor Harry ! Harry would put his hand in his pocket and feel a horrid, wretched little cherry stone ; he would open one of his school books, and a cherry stone would fall out ; he would find a cherry stone lying on his desk in the school room, until the poor boy was literally dreaming of cherry stones ! This treatment at last so got on his nerves that he did the wisest thing he could do, he owned up, and took his punishment like a man !

But again, it is happier to think not so much of the sin but of the virtue. What a fine thing it is to be honest, to have no pain in the conscience, or shame in the eye, to feel that you have played squarely with everybody.

It is a good thing to remember that a strong self-control, and simple living help very much to deliver us from the temptation to be dishonest.

There is a fine story told of a Roman General who had led the armies of Rome victoriously against their fierce foes, the Sammites. This General lived very simply and quietly in a little cottage just outside the wall of Rome, and one night, in the darkness, certain spies came to his dwelling and offered him a heap of shining gold to betray his cause. The General at the moment was heating a pot of onion porridge on a little fire for his supper. As he poured the onion porridge into the bowl, he turned to these men and said : ' A General who can make a supper of onion porridge does not require your gold. Go ! ' And he kept his honour unstained.

One of the saddest forms of dishonesty to-day is gambling, the attempt to win a bigger sum of money from somebody else by the trifle which is sacrificed. Just now vast sums of money are tempting many people to this kind of sin, and our newspapers are, alas, full of this particular temptation. Christian boys and girls must have nothing whatever to do with it because it is only a rather more polite form of stealing. It means that all the little sums given by a great number of people come to you if you win, and they really cannot afford to lose the money, they begrudge you the large amount you have won, so that envy and bitterness is created in their hearts as well as greed, and the winning of the money in this way is seldom a blessing to the person who wins.

The way in which we secure money has a great influence on our character. We must remember always the warning of the New Testament that the love of money is a great root of evil. The excitement of gambling can become like a drug to the soul, setting up a kind of mania for itself. Great numbers of young men and young women are being ruined by this bad habit to-day and it is well for us to be warned of it whilst we are children.

CHAPTER X

THE NINTH RULE—TRUTHFULNESS

' Thou shalt not bear false witness against thy neighbour.'

IN THE MAKING of a new nation, which was the task that Moses had in hand, it must have been of great importance that the people should be warned of the danger of telling lies about one another, since nothing breaks up a society so certainly as that kind of thing. Any widespread practice of untruthfulness means that people cannot depend upon one another, and therefore they cannot work together, and all their common life goes steadily to pieces.

Of course it is to a special form of lying that this Commandment refers, and the danger is reflected in the practice in our own Law Courts of making all witnesses promise, holding the Scriptures in their hands, that they will ' tell the truth, the whole truth, and nothing but the truth.' But it is not only in a Court of Law we should behave like that ; if we train ourselves to be scrupulously truthful we shall speak the truth if we ever come to appear as witnesses in a Law Court, and lying is just as dangerous everywhere else in life.

Someone has written ' The Natural History of a Lie ' ; I will quote just the first and last verses only :—

> First somebody told it,
> Then the room wouldn't hold it,
> For the busy tongues rolled it
>   And got it outside ;
> When the crowd came across it,
> They never once lost it,
> But tossed it and tossed it,
>   Till it grew long and wide !

At last, evil-boded,
It fretted and goaded,
Till at last it exploded
   In sin and in shame ;
While through smoke and through fire
The pieces flew higher,
Till they hit the said liar,
   And killed his good name.

Notice how the lie at last comes home to roost ! But again, it is happier for us to think of the virtue of truthfulness. Truth aims at making what is within an exact copy of what is without, so that we are not misled, and it is a thrilling thing to know that if we use our minds aright we can grow into all the truth about God, and this wonderful world, and all things whatsoever.

There was once a little Scotch fellow named Willie, who was sent away from home to a boarding school. Just before he left home his dear father had died, and almost the last thing he said to Willie was, ' My boy, always be true ; speak the truth and seek truth,' and Willie promised that he would.

He had not been in his new school more than an hour or so before he was face to face with a very severe test. He found that they had the quaint practice of allowing the boys at the end of the day to mark themselves ! As the boys' names were called, each boy had to announce the marks that he had allotted to himself. They were supposed to deduct marks for speaking, and other items of wrong behaviour during class. To Willie's astonishment, nearly everybody in the class had apparently behaved perfectly, because boy after boy sang out cheerfully in response to his name the full marks of the day—ten ! But when Willie counted up the things he had done during the day, he stammered out in response to his name—' None ! ' The teacher looked up sharply as though he had had a shock, and the other boys glared at Willie, and after school they began to abuse him. But Willie had something to say on his own account.

' I saw you talking ! ' he said to one, ' and I saw you eating sweets ! ' he said to another.

' Well,' said one of the boys, ' we should not have any marks at all if we did what you did ! '

Then Willie turned on them and asked : ' Do you think I would tell ten lies all at once ? '

He was so firm about it that the boys gave him a nickname ; they called him ' Little Scotch Granite.' But the teacher noticed that they became a little more modest in marking themselves and six, seven, eight, and sometimes five and four appeared instead of the regulation ten. The teacher said nothing, though Willie's record for the term was really deplorable.

On the last day of the term, after the marking had taken place, the teacher took out of his desk a little medal and said : ' I am going to give this medal to the boy whose marks record for the term is the lowest in the class, but I am giving it to him because of his extreme accuracy in marking, and because I think that such truthfulness deserves recognition. To whom shall I give it ? ' And with one voice the boys replied : ' To Little Scotch Granite, sir ! ' It was a very proud moment for Willie, who had felt very unhappy about the whole business, when the teacher pinned that medal on his coat—for truthfulness !

It is worth remembering what a mess our world would be in if it were not for accuracy or truthfulness ; if ships and trains and bridges were built just anyhow ; if pounds and ounces were wrongly measured ; if clocks always told the wrong time, and the compass began to lark about ! Surely in such a world as this, where so much safety and happiness depend upon true things, it is most important that boys and girls should be truthful too.

We ought to remember the great numbers of brave men and women who, generation by generation, have given their lives in martyrdom for what they felt to be true, who in spite of danger, of not only the threat but the ugly presence of cruel death, kept their souls incorruptible and yielded up their lives as torches of light to lighten the path of mankind. We think of such men as Ridley and Latimer being burnt at the stake at Oxford, and Latimer's great words about lighting a candle that day which could never be put out :—

> Ah ! little they knew who lit that fire
> And wrought, as they thought, their fell desire,
> That they kindled another unquenchable flame
> Which for ages and ages should burn the same,
> A beacon light on the pathway trod
> By English souls in their quest of God.
>
> Latimer's light shall never go out
> However the winds shall blow it about,
> Latimer's light is here to stay
> Till the dawn of the coming Judgement Day.

Take care of the light that is in you, boys and girls, the light of Truth.

CHAPTER XI

THE TENTH RULE—CONTENTMENT

*' Thou shalt not covet thy neighbour's house, thou shalt
not covet thy neighbour's wife, not his manservant, nor
his maidservant, nor his ox, nor his ass, nor anything
that is thy neighbour's.'*

ALMOST AS IMPORTANT in the making of a nation as
truthfulness is this habit of contentment, which keeps
folk from envying and coveting the well-being of their
neighbours. The word ' covet ' just means simply
' to desire.' Sometimes it is used in a good sense as,
for example, when St. Paul tells us to ' covet earnestly
the best gifts.' But in this Commandment it is used in
the bad sense, and means to desire so strongly as to be
touched with ill-will. It is a spirit that may so easily
lead to the breaking of some others of these rules, like
the rule of self-control, or the rule of honesty. It is a
wretched spirit that cannot rejoice in the prosperity and
happiness of others, and so often it seizes upon folk who
are not so clever and efficient and industrious as others.
It springs from a secret feeling of unworthiness, and it is
this self-anger which gets directed against the more
fortunate folk. It means the presence in our minds
of a greediness which refuses to pay the price in effort
or carefulness that might improve our own condition,
and it can become a desperately unhappy state to be in.

How much wiser it is to count our own blessings and
rejoice in what we have. St. Paul said once ' Contentment with Godliness is great gain.' It is a mean spirit,
after all, which cannot see somebody else's beautiful

47

garden without wanting it for oneself, or that feels it must say unkind things about people who have been promoted to higher positions than oneself. It is well to remember that when we start desiring greedily we begin an appetite that nothing can really satisfy. When we have gained one thing we want another, and as fast as we obtain it we grow discontented again, and there is no end to the business.

There is a rather terrible story in the Book of Kings telling us how Ahab, the King, cast covetous eyes upon the vineyard that belonged to Naboth the Jezreelite ; but Naboth loved his beautiful grape garden and would not give it up to the King. Then the wicked Queen made a plot against Naboth, in which she persuaded certain nobles to bear false witness against Naboth, so that he was at last condemned and stoned to death. But Elijah got to hear of this, and with wonderful courage went forth to meet Ahab the King and denounced him for his wickedness, telling him he had sold himself ' to work evil in the sight of the Lord.' Then the story goes on to tell us of the terrible fate that befell the evil Queen—' the dogs shall eat Jezebel by the wall of Jezreel.' It is a sad story, but it shows us how the sin of covetousness leads to the sin of falsehood and the sin of murder.

Now let us turn from the sin and consider the virtue. When you are older you will perhaps read a book by David Grayson called *Adventures in Contentment*. In this book Mr. Grayson tells of meeting a millionaire— a Mr. Starkweather—who owns a stately old house, surrounded by lovely lawns, drives, and walks, and has the finest horses in the country. Listen to the description of this millionaire : ' He had a rich look ; he walked rich, there was richness in the confident crook of his elbow, and in the positive twitch of the stick he carried ! ' But Mr. Grayson does not covet the rich man's possessions, indeed he wonders sometimes whether the millionaire inside his fences gets as much joy out of his property as the man who walks the road outside.

It is amusing to read of their meeting. One day Mr. Grayson was repairing his farm wagon when the millionaire appeared on the scene. The two men exchange greetings, and Mr. Starkweather is astounded by the request to ' take hold of the axle and steady it ! ' This was not the kind of treatment usually meted out to him. People were always so ready to flatter him and treat him with great respect, just *because* he was rich. The expression on his face seemed to imply, ' Perhaps you don't know who I am ! ' but Mr. Grayson goes on calmly, ' You take hold there, and I'll get hold here, and together we will easily get the wheel off.' And before he quite realizes what is happening, Mr. Starkweather finds himself working, actually working hard and enjoying it ! When the job is finished the two men talk. Mr. Starkweather cannot understand why a man like Mr. Grayson is content to be ' only a farmer,' and points out the advantages of being a millionaire. But Mr. Grayson is not at all impressed, and in his turn points out that he has a ' good cornfield, a cow, a horse, and a few pigs, a comfortable home, and plenty of food.' He ' enjoys the beauty of the mornings and evenings, and some of the neighbours have become his good friends.' And he asks : ' Would I be any better off, or any happier, if I had fifty thousand a year ? '

Mr. Starkweather laughs, and says he does not believe Mr. Grayson would have any truer friends, although he cannot agree with all that the other has said, and soon the conversation ends.

Boys and girls so often want very much to be rich that it will be well to remember this story to learn the deep meaning of this great rule of life—Contentment.

D

Chapter XII

THE GREATEST RULE OF LIFE—LOVE

' A new Commandment I give unto you, That ye love one another as I have loved you, that ye also love one another.'

' A NEW COMMANDMENT I give unto you,' said Jesus, ' that ye love one another.' If we truly love, we shall not fail in any one of these Commandments. We shall want to bring to those we love nothing but good, never evil, and loving God we shall make Him the one and only supreme affection of our lives.

Let us think first of all how wonderfully Jesus fulfilled His own command. Christmas tells us of the way in which the Son of God came from Heaven, with all its glory, to become a little baby, amidst all the perils and difficulties and temptations of earth, and how He lived the life of a little child, then of a lad, and at last of a grown man, so that He might show to us and to every one the marvellous beauty and the perfect loyalty of the Love Divine. Whenever we feel ourselves failing in love, we must turn to Jesus and refresh our enthusiasm for the greatest Commandment of all. Nothing is more beautiful than the way in which the Christmas season opens the hearts of all people to love, the way in which everybody starts making tender and often costly sacrifices to ensure the happiness of one another at Christmas time.

You will all remember how the people brought gifts to the little Baby in the Manger, but I wonder whether any of you know the legend of how the trees loved Him too, and planned to give their gifts ?

Around the Manger grew the palm tree, and the olive, and the fir, and on the night when Jesus was born they began to talk to each other. ' A little Baby has been born in that Manger, to bring Peace to the earth,' said the palm tree, ' and wise men are bringing Him their gifts. I will give Him a present too, He shall have my leaves and His Mother can use them to fan Him in the hot weather.'

' Yes,' answered the olive tree, ' and I, also, will give Him a gift. He shall have my oil, and His Mother can use it to heal and strengthen Him.'

Then they both looked at the fir tree—it was only a very little tree, and the palm and olive felt quite superior as they said, ' *You* have no gift to give to the Christ Child, you would only hurt Him with your prickly branches ! ' And the tiny fir tree was very sad because it knew it had nothing to offer to the Baby Jesus.

But in the shadow of the trees stood an Angel who had listened to all that had been said, and now He came out and looking up at the sky He said, ' My stars, you have heard what the palm and the olive have planned, and you see the fir tree is sad because it has no gift to give to the Christ Child. Will you come down and hang yourselves on its branches ? ' And the stars answered joyfully, ' Yes, we will do that ! ' Then one by one the beautiful stars dropped softly through the sky down to the little fir tree until each of its branches shone with their glory. The Angel opened the door of the Manger, and when the little Baby awoke in the night He saw His first Christmas Tree ! And to this day the fir tree is used at Christmas time to bring joy to every little child.

There is a beautiful story told of a brother and sister who were left without parents in a little Canadian town, and who were very poor. The brother was a cripple and found it difficult to get about, and the sister was a great lover of music, and she and her brother stinted themselves in order that she might have valuable violin lessons.

It was getting towards Christmas, and both of these brave little people had made up their minds to make a special sacrifice for each other. The brother had made up his mind to sell his two lovely dogs, to give his sister a Christmas present of a new and really good violin. And all the time she was planning to sell her old violin and give up her music lessons in order to buy him a dog sleigh so that he could travel about quite easily.

Two days before Christmas there was a terrible snow storm in their neighbourhood, and late at night a weary old traveller came knocking at their door, very spent with the storm, and told how his little car was jammed in the snow some miles away and he had wandered on seeking some habitation. He was very exhausted and ill because the exposure had done him harm. The brother and sister took him in for the night and gave him food, and, when he recovered, in a most amusing way each confided to him the wonderful secret about the Christmas present for the other. They nursed the old man through the next day and then got him back to his car, and he resumed his journey to the big city not so far away.

Both the brother and sister made mysterious journeys to the big city too, on the same day. The cripple lad took his dogs with him, for company he said, and got back home so late that his sister was in bed, so she did not see he was without the dogs on his return, or the mysterious parcel he carried under his arm.

On the Christmas morning, the sister gave to the brother a beautiful sleigh, and he gave to her a new violin, and they did not know whether to laugh or cry!

He had a sleigh and no dogs, and she had a violin and no money for lessons! And whilst they were half-laughing and half-crying, so happy were they in each other's love and sacrifice, and yet so pathetic at what they had lost, there came a knock at the door and there was their friend to whom they had played the Good Samaritan ; and he had with him the two dogs the lad had sold, and a whole year's promise of lessons from a fine violin teacher for the girl, as his contribution to their Christmas happiness.

It is not always that love and self-sacrifice are so swiftly rewarded, but I think you and I can be glad that it was so in this case. The greatest joy of all, however, for that brother and sister was found in the wonderful revelation of the perfect love they had for one another. I think Christ must have been wonderfully present in that home on that Christmas Day, and those young people would understand all afresh certain beautiful words that St. John wrote once : ' He that dwelleth in love dwelleth in God.'

I hope all boys and girls will take this greatest of all Commandments, the happiest of all the Rules of Life, deep into their hearts once and for all, for ' He that dwelleth in love, dwelleth in God.'

PART II

OTHER RULES OF WISDOM

Chapter I

A GOOD BEGINNING

' The fear of the Lord is the beginning of Wisdom.'

FOLK ARE RATHER FOND of quoting proverbs to boys and girls, are they not? How wise mother looks when she shakes her head at Lucy and says ' A stitch in time saves nine ! ' How dreadfully superior auntie sounds when she remarks, for Jack to overhear, ' You can take a horse to the water, but you can't make him drink ! ' You are the horse, eh? Or, when father comes home late and finds you still up, ' Early to bed, early to rise,' he says, with such an air of never ever having sat up late himself, ' makes a man healthy, wealthy, and wise.'

But of course, the most famous proverbs in the world are to be found in the Bible. So highly did the Jews value these sayings of wisdom that they gathered them carefully into a book called Proverbs. We are going to look at some of the best of these sayings. They will help to make our lives a good deal happier if we follow them out.

And so, first, for a good beginning. ' Well begun is half done,' says an English proverb, and this first choice of ours from the Book of Proverbs tells us that wisdom begins in ' the fear of the Lord.'

Now, this word ' fear ' does not mean here ' being afraid.' It cannot mean that for Christian boys and girls, because Jesus taught us never to be afraid of God, but always to trust and love Him. It means ' reverence ' —a deep and awed respect. Reverent fear, or the fear that is tender, loving reverence, is what we should all feel at the approach of Christ. This trembling wondering awe which yet does not make us afraid is ' the fear of the Lord ' which is ' the beginning of wisdom.'

Perhaps the best way of getting at the richest meaning of this proverb is to remember a beautiful description of God, given to us in the New Testament, ' God is Love.' To reverence love is the beginning of being wise.

There is a fine story, told by Robert Morris, of a ship's captain named Neil Cameron who came from the Highlands of Scotland. Unhappily, he cared not at all for the beauty of mountain and glen, but only for gold. Wherever his ship went he sought for gold, and still more gold. It was his only dream and delight. Whenever he could load his ship with gold, he would sail away and hide it in a treasure cave on an island of the southern sea.

Neil Cameron had run away from home, and so full of greed of gold was he, that never had he given a thought even to that cottage in the bleak Highlands where, in a pine tree by the door, a grey homing dove had her nest. Often as a lad he had listened to the grey dove's soft cooing, and always it had seemed to say to him, ' Co-me ho-me ! Co-me ho-me ! ' Then one day he came sailing to his treasure cave and found nothing there ! An earthquake had shaken the cliff and cave to pieces and buried his treasure for ever. Neil Cameron fell into such a terrible rage, when he found out his loss, that his men fled from him in fear and left him on the island.

When his madness was spent, there came to him a dream. A man with shining wings stood before him and inquired about his trouble. Neil told him of his loss, and with a strange smile, the stranger waved a wand in the air, and a door appeared. ' If you will give up all other dreams and wishes and enter this door, you can have more than you have lost, and the ruling of the world,' he said. Cameron was about to step through that door when suddenly, ' Coo ! coo ! coooo ! ' came the voice of a dove to him, and in a flash he knew that deeper than his longing for gold was his desire for love. Neil turned to his angel-visitor and cried, ' Oh, stay ! Instead of gold give me—for I am not worthy to have my home again—give me but one feather from the breast of that grey dove that nests by the old front door.' Again the stranger smiled and disappeared.

When Neil lifted his eyes, a ship stood in the bay, and after a long journey the wanderer was walking once more up the path that led to that old cottage door. The first thing he saw was the grey dove flitting through the twilight to its nest, then he heard its gentle ' Co-me ho-me ! ' and his mother was standing in the doorway—an old, old woman now, but with love still shining in her eyes. In a moment he was in her arms, and knew, once for all, that Love is the only real treasure.

CHAPTER II

KEEPING IT UP

' In all thy ways acknowledge Him, and He shall direct thy paths.'

IT IS NOT OF MUCH USE beginning well unless we can keep it up. If reverence for God and for what is holy is the beginning of wisdom, the steady habit of reckoning with God in all our thoughts and actions is the continuance of wisdom.

There used to be in Edinburgh a very well-known professor who was renowned for the fact that he always wore an old plaid shawl. However fine his clothes might be, and whatever the important occasion he might be attending, he always wore the ' auld plaid shawl.' This he did in loving memory of his mother—a simple working woman, by whose patient sacrifice her son had secured a good education. His pride was so great in being her son ! We may be sure that in this way the spirit of his mother was always with him, keeping him fine and noble amidst the many temptations of life. His acknowledgment of his mother gave her power to direct his ways.

This is something of the meaning of this noble proverb. You and I must never be ashamed to acknowledge God. It is a strange thing, but sometimes boys and girls are ashamed to do this. Sometimes they find themselves with other children who do not think of God, whose parents have allowed them to grow up with hardly a thought of Him. Some children never pray themselves, and look scornfully upon those who do. In this way you may sometimes be tempted to lie low about your own habit of prayer or belief in or reverence of God. You do not like to stand out as different from the others, and you feel shy about being called religious or ' soppy ' or ' pi,' as some folk call it. But all that is very unworthy. If you believe that God has made this beautiful world, has given you life with all its treasures of joy and friendship, it is simply a cad's trick to be in any way ashamed of such a friend. You would not dream of being afraid to acknowledge your mother or father or sister, or your best friend, yet here is One without whom these others simply would not be !

There is a noble and true Quaker story of a man named Leonard Fell, who, riding one April night through a wooded valley, was held up by a highwayman. The highwayman, seizing the rein of Mr. Fell's horse with one hand and presenting his pistol with the other, cried fiercely, ' Your money, or I shoot ! ' To his amazement, the rider replied quite calmly, ' Here is my purse, containing all that I have with me except some money in my new saddle-bag. A neighbour's wife gave me that for calico I am to buy for her.' As the highwayman released the horse to hold out his hand for the purse, the horse tossed her head and knocked the pistol out of his hand. All this time the thief had felt the uncanny calm of his victim, and had made up his mind that it was a strong and fearless man with whom he had to do, who was biding his time. So the highwayman was now in a panic, but hoped that in the darkness his victim had not noticed the fall of the pistol.

' Get off your horse, or I'll shoot it from under you ! ' the highwayman cried, leaping to the side of the road as the horse pranced on the spot where the weapon lay. ' On the instant, I tell you ! '

The rider pulled down his horse, sat motionless for a breathless moment, then swung himself down slowly, without a word. The robber darted forward, leaped into the saddle and jerked the horse, about to make his escape before his uncanny victim should open fire. A hand on the reins stopped him, and to his amazement the man said :

'I have given thee what thou asked for, but thou wilt have to render account of it before God. By the holy Light that shines within each one of us, how dost thou dare to ignore thy Master's voice, pleading with thee to turn aside from the paths of evil to follow Him ? '

The tension broke as the highwayman realized with anger that the man instead of resisting was preaching to him. All the bitterness of his life spoke in his snarl. 'Loose the reins and hold thy tongue, or I'll blow your brains out ! '

'Nay, friend, thy weapon lies in the dirt. But though I would not give my life for my money or my horse, I would give it to save thy soul ! '

The highwayman was struck by a new and almost unbelievable thought. This man knew before he dismounted that the pistol had fallen ; he had every advantage with which to either strike or flee, and yet he had quietly given what was asked with no sign of fear—indeed, he spoke almost with gentleness. Could it be God, of whom the highwayman had not thought for years, was speaking to him ? In a swift panic he leaped from the horse, pressed the wallet, with a hurried 'Take it, take it ! ' into the good man's hands, and turning, plunged down the road, but as he ran he heard : 'Mayest thou receive guidance from above, and if I, Leonard Fell, can do aught to aid thee . . . ' He ran on, but despair had left him. He became suddenly aware of a strange stirring in his soul that somehow seemed in harmony with the beauty of the night.

Thus did Leonard Fell bravely acknowledge God in face of a highway robber's threats, and God certainly ' directed his paths.'

Will you do this as opportunity offers, and so ' keep it up ' ?

Chapter III

THE LIGHTED WAY

' *The path of the righteous is as the shining light, shining more and more to the perfect day.*'

IF OUR PROVERBS have really guided us so far we should be stepping out bravely along the ' lighted way.' What a wonderful and lovely thing is light. Have you ever had a long, dark journey in the country and then caught sight of the light of home ? Or have you ever had a wakeful night, and stared out into the darkness hour after hour, and then caught the first gleams of the rosy light of dawn ? It is easy to see why light stands for goodness and darkness for evil, is it not ? Light is so good in itself, whilst somehow darkness always seems to encourage the worst in us. ' How oft the means to do ill deeds make ill deeds done,' says Shakespeare, and darkness is such a means. Then, too, the soul that does wrong grows dark. It becomes confused in its outlook and judgement—it becomes full of gloom and shadow ; whilst the soul that does right grows light. Conscience is easy and honour shines upon the way of life—the eye and the step are bright with the sense of God's favour. It is the lighted way. Keep this light of the soul, which is goodness, always shining, dear boys and girls. Never let it be put out.

Many years ago there was a noted knight of the famous city of Florence, named Raniero de Raniero, who had earned the character of a very proud and cruel tyrant. He set out with a great company upon one of those Crusades that took the flower of European chivalry to the Holy Land. So selfish and hard was he that even his beautiful wife, Francesca, was not quite sorry when he said goodbye to her. Before he went, Raniero knelt before the altar of the proudest church in Florence and vowed before the congregation to bring back to his native city *the most precious thing he could find.*

When at last the company reached Jerusalem and laid siege to the city, Raniero was second only to Godfrey of Boulogne, the leader, in deeds of courage.

To Raniero, as a reward for his prowess, had been given the privilege of being first to light his taper from the flame that burned before the sacred tomb of Christ. There was no clank of armour, only the soft footfall of this company of knights, who were clad in the garb of penitents, but who were, so many of them, proud and hard of heart. Raniero, at their head, paced up the dark aisle toward the sacred flame. Now, when he saw that flame burning in his taper, he knew that here was the most precious thing he could find in the Holy Land.

So next morning, resisting temptation to stay, and clad in armour over which he had thrown a heavy cloak, with sword and battle-axe, and a great bundle of extra tapers to feed his flame, he started on his homeward pilgrimage with the burning candle in his hand. He soon realized that he could not go very swiftly—the little light wavered and he must needs draw his horse to a walk that it might flare up again.

One day, when passing through a wild and lonely defile, he saw before him a band of robbers. They were few and poorly armed, and his first thought was to gallop through them striking right and left with his huge sword, but no—the little light was far too frail for such a venture, and proud Raniero rode slowly into the midst of the robber band and said : ' Friend, take what you will, but do not harm my light.'

E

Amazed, they took from him his horse, money, armour, sword, till nothing was left him but the heavy cloak and the burning taper. On leaving, the leader of the band, touched, perhaps, by his sad plight, called ' Take my horse, 'tis fast enough to carry a candle ! ' and with mocking laughter they rode away.

Once on a lonely mountain path a woman ran from a cottage, calling : ' Stranger, give me, I pray you, light from your candle. My fire has gone out, and I can bake no bread for my children.'

' No, no,' said Raniero, ' the light I carry is too sacred for common use. I cannot give it to you.'

But the woman cried : ' The light I would guard is my children's lives—it will not lessen your flame to give it to me ! '

So Raniero lighted her lamp, and it seemed to him that his flame burned more brightly.

But that night, on the mountains, a terrible storm of wind and rain put the little light out. At first, utterly discouraged, he sank upon the wet ground, but he suddenly cried, with relief : ' The woman's light is the sacred flame ! By giving, I have saved it ! ' And he hastened back to the cottage.

Other adventures he had, which would take too long to tell. At last he came to the outskirts of Florence, and the people marvelled at the weather-beaten man on the gaunt old horse, ragged and tattered and carrying a lighted candle ! The crowd followed him, growing larger as crowds will, and changing from laughter and wonder to jeers and threats.

' Put out his light ! Put out his light ! ' they cried, trying to reach his taper. Raniero, desperate, struggled on. He held the light high, searching the jeering faces before him for some understanding response. Suddenly, from a balcony above him, a woman leaned over and snatched the burning candle, and the crowd, shrieking with laughter, hooted afresh as Raniero fell fainting on the road.

When he opened his eyes again he saw, bending over him, his wife Francesca, who, alone of all the multitude, had recognized him. ' I took the light,' she said, ' I am guarding it.' Understanding love had once again saved the flame.

Together they took the candle to the church, and Raniero recounted to the priest the tale of his long pilgrimage, and had the joy of placing on the altar the little light he had grown so much to love.

And the priest, with bowed head, said ' God grant we may keep the Sacred Flame burning in Florence ! '

What about your own Sacred Flame ?

CHAPTER IV

DOING DOES IT

' *Go to the ant, thou sluggard, consider her ways and be wise.* '

To LIVE THROUGH a whole year well and nobly means that one must be ready and eager at one's work. So much of our life is taken up at first with preparing for the work of the world, and later in doing it. Said a man once, who is one of the hardest workers I know, ' The only way I keep myself from laziness is to work as hard as I possibly can.' He knows that ' doing does it.' Doing is not only a remedy for laziness ; it is a remedy for all other ills, too. An active person not only keeps in better health of body, but in better health of mind and soul as well. The hours of idleness are the danger hours of life.

' Go to the ant ' is good advice for all who would be inspired in their work, for the ants are mighty workers. Their industry in all kinds of toil is amazing. There are ' carpenter-ants ' who are not content with earthen homes, but who cut wood and smooth or plane it and floor their rooms, and build in this way storey upon storey of real sky-scraper buildings ! Others are mason ants who build their cities of stone and earth, cemented by the moisture from their lips.

These mason and carpenter-ants seem to be very keen rivals and often fight. The carpenters are big, the masons small, and a gentleman who once witnessed a fight between them has left a very interesting record of it. He tells us that it began by half-a-dozen ' carpenters ' setting upon a group of the small ' masons ' about twelve noon one day. One of the mason ants, however, escaped, and crawled back to its city at the foot of an apple tree. By one o'clock long lines of ant-troops were pouring forth from that city and advancing upon the city of the carpenter-ants. That, too, poured forth its army, and a great battle took place. The little masons at the moment of attack changed their formation into groups of six. Each group marched for one of the giant ants. One seized the antenæ, others the legs, and two leapt upon its back and another crept beneath it and stabbed a vital spot. Every big carpenter-ant, it seemed, was slain in this war, the mason-ants being in superior numbers. The silent city, which had been entirely wrecked, seemed just a cemetery of the dead, when the masons marched away victoriously.

But as the man watched, he saw a big carpenter-ant struggle up out of the debris. She was carrying in her mouth a tiny cradle containing a baby ant. It was very heavy, but though distracted by fear and exhausted with her struggles, she never forsook her charge. Away into the woods and the night she stumbled, to breed perhaps a new race of giant ants to avenge the fallen.

At least we may learn something of the splendid energy of the ant from that account from real life. No creatures are so human in their behaviour as these wonderful though tiny insects. They show energy of mind as well as of body, and will constantly find quick and clever solutions of difficulties. A friend of mine once watched an ant struggling with a straw which was, of course, many times longer than itself. He dragged it and pushed it until at last he was stopped by a bad break in the ground. The ant stopped to think. It extended too far for him to think of working round it. But presently he calmly pushed the long straw across the opening, crawled across on the straw, and then pulled it after him. He had turned his burden into a bridge ! There is a lesson for us all. Doing does it ! Do not fret and fume at the burdens and difficulties of life— *tackle them,* and they will prove ever so much easier than at first they appear.

There are some ants called ' bridge makers ' who show wonderful intelligence. In order to ford a river they link themselves together into a continuous chain—ever so light. One end of the chain then surrenders itself to the wind, and that end floats on the wind across the gulf that is to be spanned, and over that living bridge the rest of the company cross to safety. Then all those who have gone over unite their strength to those who first arrive and so pull the living bridge on the new side of the gulf. Isn't that clever ?

If only we would all learn the art of working together, then ' doing ' would do it indeed. This is what Jesus is working for. He wants all His followers to love each other so truly that they behave as one family. That is the way to get the greatest things done ! Not till the people of all nations really pull together can we put an end to poverty and to war and to slavery and to famine. We need to make a ' loop of life ' round the whole earth in order at last to ' do ' the deeds God wants done. Will you help ?

Chapter V

KEEPING TRUE

' A false balance is an abomination to the Lord, but a just weight is His delight.'

WHEN PEOPLE ARE VERY POOR, as many of the Jews were, it is a matter of great importance indeed that in their buying they should get fair treatment, and no meaner trick could be thought of or done, than to use scales that were wrongly balanced in serving to the poor the necessities of life. But all of us are merchants in some sense—going to one another for truth, and weighing truth out to each other. There are many ways of being false, and they are all mean. We do not always realize how dependent our safety and happiness are upon simple truth. Suppose trolleys and trams and trains were not built in strict accord with accuracy, namely truth, how quickly accidents and disasters would prove to us truth's value ! It is a dreadful thing when we feel we cannot trust those about us, and hence, elsewhere in Scripture we are told that ' a lie is an abomination unto the Lord.' The Lord hates such things because they do such dreadful harm to His human children whose safety and happiness are so dear to Him.

You have heard of the famous Kodak cameras—perhaps you have one ? Well, here is the fine story of George Eastman, the Kodak man. When he started, cameras were fearfully heavy and clumsy things, and having to do some photographs while travelling, he grew so tired of carrying the big, heavy plates required, that he determined to invent something lighter and handier, and he did.

For a long time he worked far into the night to invent a dry plate easy to carry. After two years he succeeded. He left his employment as a bank clerk to give himself up to the making of these plates. Large quantities were distributed to a host of customers. But after a short time it was found that the chemicals on these plates failed to retain their virtue—the gelatine on them dried up and the plates lost their sensitiveness.

When George Eastman heard of this, he took every plate and refunded every penny paid for them, though it left him a ruined man. With splendid courage he said : ' I will find out what is wrong.' So hard was life whilst ' finding out ' that his hair turned grey. But, although he and his family were brought almost to starvation, George Eastman would not sell a worthless article. At last he found out the cause of the trouble and patented his famous transparent film, which led on to the discovery of cinema pictures. His splendid honesty found a great reward, and to-day there is one Kodak factory alone in America which employs 20,000 men, and nearly a quarter of a million miles of cinema films are manufactured by the Kodak Company every year.

George Eastman knew the glory of truth and held to it with all his might, with the result that he has brought pleasure and a deep happiness to millions of his fellows.

Beware of the lies of behaviour as well as those of speech. To allow people to be under a false impression, and perhaps to build their conduct upon it, when it is in your power to put them right, is deeply wrong, and may do quite as much harm as speaking an untruth.

A youth once was engaged in carrying heavy planks of timber from a timber yard to a boat on the river. They were to be used in the building of a great bridge, and, to spite the manager of the yard, a foreman passed one or two rotten planks and would hear no protest from this young man. For days those rotten planks burdened his conscience. He could see them being built into that bridge and bringing at last untold disaster upon those who used it. But the responsibility was not his, it was the foreman's. Yet could he really argue like that? At last he went straight to the Head of the company, and told his story, and the consignment of planks was held up before they were used and the bad pieces thrown out. Every one was grateful that the youth had found the courage to tell the truth at the risk of being told to mind his own business, and being dismissed. 'I am my brother's keeper,' and I must never play him false.

Beware then, boys and girls, of anything false in any part of your life.

A man once set out to build a wall, and in a careless moment allowed one brick to lie out of the straight. He took his line for the rest of the bricks in the row from that one falsely laid brick. At first it did not make much difference, but, as the rows of bricks were piled higher and higher upon that false line, the tilt became increased and one morning, after a night of storm, he came to his work to find it lying in ruins upon the ground. That which is untrue cannot stand for ever ; it is ' an abomination to the Lord.'

' The Settler's Wife,' tells of the sad trouble that came from the hasty tongue of a thoughtless and angry man. He says in the poem :

> Boys flying kites haul in their white-winged birds,
>   You can't do that way when you're flying words ;
> Thoughts unexpressed may sometimes fall back dead,
>   But God Himself can't kill them once they're said.

Healthy speech ! Never unclean nor impure ! Don't soil your mouth with dirty swear-words, boys and (yes, I am sorry I must say it) girls ! Often you do not know the meaning of such horrible words, so leave them unsaid, please. If you saw a little boy who had fallen in the mud, and was plastered from head to feet with it, you would hasten to help him, wouldn't you ? You would wipe the mud from his mouth and eyes as quickly as you could. Well, it would do that friend of yours good if, the next time you heard him swear you took your handkerchief (a clean one, I hope !) and gently wiped his lips for him !

Healthy speech ! Praise be for the jolly humorous folk who ' greet the unseen with a cheer,' and have a joke ready when things are dull and life is hard. Praise be for those who know how to speak calmly and quietly when everybody else is excited and has the ' jim-jams,' as we say. Praise be for those who speak, at the right moment, a brave word for Christ, and turn another life out of the wrong road on to the right one. Truly, as this delightful Book of Proverbs says in another place :

> 'A word fitly spoken is like apples of gold
>   in baskets of silver.'

CHAPTER VII

ANSWERING BACK

'A soft answer turneth away wrath.'

THIS PROVERB hits at a difficulty that we all know very well. That rush of hot speech, to which most of us are inclined when we are spoken to roughly or angrily, is not easy to hold back. ' I gave him as good as I got ! ' Who has not heard that boast? But supposing what you ' got ' was itself bad, how ' good ' was your reply after all? It really does take two to make a quarrel. If only we could all remember that, there would be very few quarrels at all.

One of the best and wittiest ' soft answers ' to ' wrath ' was that given by the famous Greek philosopher, Epictetus, when he was attacked by someone who criticized his character. The philosopher quietly replied, ' Ah, yes, alas ! that is not the only fault either, there is this, and that,' and he went on to mention other failings of his, so humbly and with such sincere sorrow, that his critic was left speechless. It is not all of us who can muster as much humility as that.

Sir Bartle Frere, when he was Governor of Sind, in India, was once thrown from his horse and badly bruised through a Hindu, who had been waiting to present his case to the Governor, suddenly rising to his feet from beside the pathway leading to the Governor's house, and so startling the horse. When Sir Bartle had picked himself up, he turned calmly to the Hindu who was desperately frightened at the accident, and asked quietly, ' My son, why did you stand up like that?' The

CHAPTER VIII

MIND YOUR STEP

' Pride goeth before a fall.'

' OH ! HE'S SO STUCK UP, I don't like him ! ' ' Look at her ! Doesn't she hold her nose in the air ? ' Have you ever heard things like that said, or said them ? The idea in these well-known ways of speech is the same as in the proverb. The proud person keeps his head so high in the air that he cannot see where his feet are going ! As a result he tumbles over !

Pride causes us to stumble for three very good reasons :—

Pride blunts the mind. It betrays the mind and kills aspiration. No one becomes so ignorant as he who *will not* learn, and no one is quite so lost as he who is so sure that he is on the right road that he will not consider any other way.

Pride closes the heart. Its attitude is one of contempt towards others. It never gives enough room and weight to their opinion. This leads to a great and sad self-centredness, and the needs of others make very little appeal. One can see this hardness of heart reflected in the sneering contemptuous gaze of the proud.

Pride weakens the will. The proud person is so content that he attempts little or nothing. There is no striving for improvement and so the power to choose and decide grows flabby.

All these things make mistakes easy and a tumble likely. That is a good thing. It may not be pleasant to fall, but it does wake you up and save you from living in a 'fool's paradise.' It is very wonderful how every evil seems to carry in its consequences that which corrects it.

The word 'Pride' in its root-meaning has the sense of 'ornamentation,' and we all know how often it shows itself in a love of jewellery and finery—vanity of dress and of appearance. The mischief, however, is that pride is always much more interested in 'putting on' and in 'appearance' than it is in actual character and real being. 'What do I look like?' is its favourite question, not 'What am I really?' It is a mistake to think that pride is the sin only of those who are rich and highly placed.

'I am the king of the Forest!' roared a lion as he sprang out of the bushes into a clearing. All would have been well if the gnat sleeping on a leaf had not heard him. 'Oh, indeed!' said the little gnat, 'let us see!' and he stung the lion neatly in the middle of his back. Angrily, the great beast lashed with his long tail, but by this time the gnat was on the tip of the lion's rather fat nose. Viciously the great jaws snapped— just too late, and the sting found his right eyebrow. So the fight went on—the gnat always alighting just where the lion thought he wasn't! Nor did the gnat leave the fierce beast until it slunk away from the field of battle with its tail between its legs, thoroughly crest-fallen.

I remember once being with a party of people on holiday. We had been for a long and tiring tramp in the morning over the hills and a friend of mine under-took to lead us home by a short cut. He kept priming us that at the top of a certain high hill, just over the brow of it, we should find our hotel and the dinner we all wanted so badly. Hopefully we toiled upward. But alas, when we reached the top, yet another great valley and high hill lay between us and our resting place.

My friend, in his pride of leadership, had mistaken the hill, misled by the fact that there were two golf-courses and not one in that district. He was sport enough to apologize for his blunder and the pride that had gone before his fall.

between ? It is so, and the reason is that too much or too little both tend to take our thoughts away from God and the soul

In the Old Testament we read of a man named Gehazi. He was Elisha's servant, and when the prophet refused to accept a gift from Naaman the Syrian for healing him of leprosy, Gehazi thought in his greed to take advantage of the fact. You remember, perhaps, how he ran after Naaman and begged a gift, and how afterwards the foolish man found he had caught the leprosy too. Thus does greed over-reach itself and turn to bigger need.

Do you remember that Jesus teaches us not to become worried about goods and clothing and shelter. We are not to go through life saying fearfully, ' What shall we eat ? What shall we drink ? How shall we be clothed ? ' To do so is to dishonour God. But He does not want us to be without these necessities, for He says ' Your Heavenly Father knoweth that ye have need of all these things,' and also ' all these things shall be added unto you.' Jesus, too, wanted us to think of God and be neither too rich nor too poor.

There were once two mice who found in the wood where they lived a fine big piece of cheese, left behind by some campers. At once each of them wanted it all. The first one claimed it because he had seen it first, but the second one claimed it, too, because he was the first to reach it. At last, not wanting to fight over it because they were very evenly matched for strength, they decided to take the cheese home and ask their friend, the wise old monkey, to decide the matter. He at once said : ' Why, of course, you must have half each,' but then he very brightly added, ' Each half must be of the same size ! ' (as if they could be halves and different !). So he took them to his wife's weighing scales, and breaking the cheese into two portions, put each piece in each of the scales. Seeing they didn't quite match, he nibbled a piece off the bigger portion. Alas ! he nibbled too much, so he hurried and bit a piece off the other. Still, they were different, so he tried again—and again— and again ! Meanwhile the two miserable mice looked on and saw their hopes of cheese steadily disappearing down the monkey's throat. At last, when the cheese was all gone, they realized that too much can come very near being too little—in fact, nothing at all !

Be wise, boys and girls, and choose, as St. Paul advises, ' moderation in all things.' Do not be too troubled because your pocket money is not enough. If it were too much you would never learn how to keep money, and very soon the biggest amount would be too little. Learn this proverb, and say it often to yourself, especially later on in life. This is one of the secrets of true happi- ness in this world—' Neither poverty nor riches—lest I forget God.'